ISLAND

a collection
jane richmond

ACKNOWLEDGMENTS

Design & Pattern Writing

Jane Richmond

Graphic Design

Shannon Cook & Jane Richmond

Photography

Nicholas Kupiak & Jane Richmond

Model

Kylee Shaw

Copyright ©2012 Jane Richmond and Marian Rae Publications

Photographs copyright ©2012 Nicholas Kupiak (pages 6-37, 60-63, and cover)
Photographs copyright ©2012 Jane Richmond (pages 38-57)
Photographs copyright ©2012 Shannon Cook (pages 59 & 64)

ISBN 978-0-9917289-0-9

Technical editing by Katherine Vaughan

CONTENTS

INTRODUCTION

by Jane Richmond

I have been self publishing my individual patterns since 2008. Putting together a collection of patterns has always been on my must-do list. What appealed to me was being able to incorporate a theme, to work with a photographer and a story board, and to create a collection with a common thread running through it.

Before I had a collection I already knew who would shoot it. Nicholas Kupiak has a way of bringing a vibrancy to his subjects. Without exception, he has the same effect on his lovely partner Kylee Shaw. Nick and Kylee have this amazing chemistry through the lens, you can tell they bring out the best in each other and that it comes so naturally. You could say that this collection was born from my desire to work with this duo on a collaboration.

Also as appealing, were all of the little extras to which the layout of a book lends itself. Each page tells a part of a larger story, and there is a flow and a direction to the artwork within the spreads. I welcomed the idea of additional physical space to tuck hints of my personality and design aesthetic into.

My first real push of moral support came from my good friend Shannon Cook of luvinthemommyhood.com. She has been a huge player in the direction of this project ever since. Shannon is one of those people that has so much creative energy that she has to have a notebook stashed in every nook and cranny of her life. Always ahead of trends and an endless source of ideas and inspiration, this book would not have been possible without her graphic design skills, knowledge of the publishing industry, and her keen eye and drive for perfection.

Publishing a collection means so much more to me than releasing a bundle of patterns. It is an opportunity for me to offer you a glimpse into where I live and what inspires me. ISLAND is a collection of pieces inspired by my life on Vancouver Island and I hope that these pages take you on a journey through a day in the life of an Islander.

FOREWORD

by Shannon Cook

I love a good story. I especially love being able to tell a story with the beauty of handmade. One of the things that I love about designing and working with others who design is "the story". I always get enchanted with dreaming up the scenarios, and there's always a back story for the characters that will wear new designs. It's one of my favorite parts of the process and one I always get super excited about.

When Jane first mentioned to me that she would like to do a collection my wheels started turning. She had no choice but to take me along for the ride and I thank her from the bottom of my heart for letting me come along. I have a love for books that goes right into my soul and it's been with me since I was a child. It's been so amazing and fun to dive headfirst into the world of book publishing & to let my imagination run wild.

Through our weekly meetings, late night coffee sessions - Jane with her Java Chip Frappuccinos and me with my Skinny Vanilla Lattes (yes, Starbucks helped us to survive), endless phone calls, creative energy & hard work, we were able to bring Jane's dream to life. It's been one of the most exciting projects I've had the pleasure of working on and I couldn't imagine having taken this journey with anyone other than Jane.

It's so rare to find a person in life that you can be both a friend and a work partner with and have them mesh so easily. As Jane and I like to say "we were meant to be friends" and you my friends, were meant to take this journey with us. So grab a mason jar, brew a cuppa tea or sip your favorite coffee, pull out that coveted yarn and curl up and knit along with us as we take you on an inspiring & special adventure on Vancouver Island.

We are so blessed to get to call this magical place home and we hope that this collection allows us to bring some of that magic into your home.

Enjoy and happy knitting!

Renfrew
page 40

Rathtrevor

page 42

Strathcona
page 44

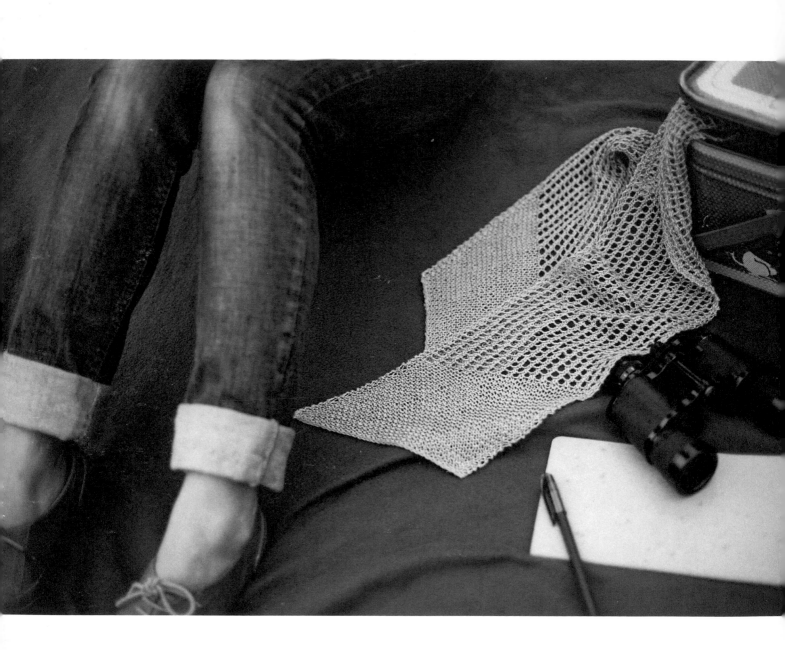

Arbutus

page 46

Grace
page 48

PATTERNS

Renfrew

This modern toque features a simple asymmetrical mock cable panel on a reverse stockinette fabric. Knit from the bottom up and inside out to maximize the use of the knit stitch. Renfrew was designed to showcase the brilliance of hand dyed, multi-faceted yarns. Shown in a slouchy style, instructions are provided for both a shorter beanie as well as this longer version to accommodate different preferences.

Gauge

19 sts and 27 rows = 4in/10cm in St st in the rnd

Yarn

1 skein Madelinetosh Tosh Vintage (100% superwash merino wool, 200yds/182m), shown in Cove [worsted]

Needles

4.5mm/US7 circular needle, 16in
4.5mm/US7 dpns

Notions

1 stitch marker
Yarn needle

Finished Measurements

Approx 18.5in/47cm circumference (unstretched) and 9.25in/23.5cm long.

Stitch Guide

yo : to yarn over between two purl stitches, bring the working yarn from front to back over the RH needle and then back to the front by coming under the RH needle.

DIRECTIONS

RIBBING

Using long tail method, CO 88 sts. Place marker and join, being careful not to twist.

Rnd 1: [P1, k1] to end of rnd.

Repeat **Rnd 1** until ribbing measures 1.5in/4cm.

BODY

Rnd 1: [P1, k1] twice, p3, [k1, p1] twice, knit to end of rnd.

Rnd 2: [P1, k1] twice, p3, pass 3rd st on RH needle over first two sts and off needle, [k1, p1] twice, knit to end of rnd.

Rnd 3: [P1, k1] twice, p2, [k1, p1] twice, knit to end of rnd.

Rnd 4: [P1, k1] twice, p1, yo, p1, [k1, p1] twice, knit to end of rnd.

Repeat **Rnds 1-4** until hat measures 7.5in/19cm from CO edge, ending with **Rnd 4**. If you prefer a fitted hat over this slouchy version work until piece measures 5.5in/14cm.

SHAPE CROWN

Change to dpns when there are too few sts to continue on circular needle.

Rnd 1: [P1, k1] twice, p3, [k1, p1] twice, [k2tog, k5] to end of rnd. 77 sts.

Rnd 2: [P1, k1] twice, p3, pass 3rd st on RH needle over first two sts and off needle, [k1, p1] twice, knit to end of rnd.

Rnd 3: Wyif skp, p1, k1, p2, k1, wyif skp, p1, [k2tog, k4] to end of rnd. 63 sts.

Rnd 4: P2, k1, p1, yo, p1, k1, p2, knit to end of rnd.

Rnd 5: P2, k1, p3, k1, p2, [k2tog, k3] to end of rnd. 53 sts.

Rnd 6: P2, k1, p3, pass 3rd st on RH needle over first two sts and off the needle, k1, p2, knit to end of rnd.

Rnd 7: P2tog, k1, p1, yo, p1, k1, p2tog, [k2tog, k2] to end of rnd. 40 sts.

Rnd 8: P1, k1, p3, k1, p1, knit to end of rnd.

Rnd 9: P1, k1, p3, pass 3rd st on RH needle over first two sts and off the needle, k1, p1, [k2tog, k1] to end of rnd. 28 sts.

Rnd 10: P1, k1, p2, k1, p1, knit to end of rnd.

Rnd 11: P1, k1, p2tog, k1, p1, [k2tog] to end of rnd. 16 sts.

Rnd 12: P2tog, p1, p2tog, knit to end of rnd. 14 sts.

Rnd 13: Wyif sp2p, [k2tog] to last st, k1. 7 sts.

Break yarn. Using yarn needle, thread through rem sts, pull tight and secure.

Weave in ends. Turn RS out.

Rathtrevor

Simple fingerless mittens with beaded ribbing ending just below the thumb gusset to create a more casual look. A quick and easy knit, this practical accessory is perfect for fall and winter. Comfortable and highly wearable, these mittens would also make great gift knitting. The pattern is written to fit an average ladies' hand and can also easily be made larger or smaller by adjusting needle size.

Gauge

22 sts and 30 rows = 4in/10cm in St st on smaller needles in the rnd

Yarn

1 skein Madelinetosh Tosh DK (100% superwash merino wool, 225yds/205m), shown in Chambray [DK]

Needles

4.5mm/US7 dpns
4mm/US6 dpns

Notions

1 removable marker
2 stitch markers
Waste yarn
Yarn needle

Finished Measurements

Approx 8.25in/21cm long and 6.75in/17cm hand circumference (unstretched).

DIRECTIONS

FOREARM

Using long tail method and larger dpns, CO 38 sts. Place removable marker and join, being careful not to twist.

Rnd 1: [K1, p1] to end of rnd.

Rnd 2: Knit.

Repeat last two rnds until forearm measures 3in/7.5cm. Change to smaller needles and continue until forearm measures 6.25in/16cm from CO edge.

SHAPE THUMB

Rnd 1: M1, k18, pm, m1, k2, m1, pm, knit to end of rnd.

Rnd 2: Knit.

Rnd 3 (Inc Rnd): knit to first marker, sm, m1, knit to second marker, m1, sm, knit to end of rnd.

Repeat last two rnds until there are 12 sts between two markers.

Next Rnd: Knit to first marker, remove marker, place 12 thumb sts onto waste yarn, remove second marker, knit to end of rnd.

Knit 7 rnds. BO.

THUMB

Place 12 thumb sts onto smaller dpns, rejoin yarn. Pick up and knit 2 sts where thumb meets hand.

Knit 6 rnds. BO.

Weave in ends.

Strathcona

A light and airy scarf knit with 100% linen for a truly all season accessory. Sloped garter ends mirror the directional lace mesh. An elongated V shape is created by using a bias stitch. Alternating the order of the stitch pattern easily shifts the direction of the knitting, creating a long scarf that echoes the shape of a triangular shawl. Perfectly portable, this project also makes excellent summer knitting.

Gauge

22 sts and 36 rows = 4in/10cm in Garter st

Yarn

2 skeins Quince & Co Sparrow (100% linen, 168yds/155m to 50g/1.76oz), shown in Blue Spruce [fingering]

Needles

4mm/US6 needles

Notions

Yarn needle

Finished Measurements

Unblocked : 36in/91.5cm long from end to center turning point and 5in/12.5cm wide

Blocked : 31in/78.5cm long from end to center turning point and 6.25in/16cm wide

DIRECTIONS

Using long tail method, CO 39. Be sure to CO loosely to maintain a stretchy edge.

RIGHT SLANTING

Garter Stitch

Row 1 (RS): K1, kfb, knit to last 3 sts, k2tog, k1.

Row 2 (WS): Knit.

Repeat **Rows 1 & 2** until garter stitch measures 6in/15cm from CO edge, ending with a **WS** row.

Next Row (Dec Row): K1, kfb, [k3, k2tog] 3 times, k4, [k2tog, k3] 3 times, k2tog, k1. 33 sts

Mesh Stitch

Row 1 (WS): K1, [k2tog, yo] to last 2 sts, k2.

Row 2 (RS): Knit.

Repeat **Rows 1 & 2** until scarf measures 36in/91.5cm from CO edge, ending with a **RS** row.

LEFT SLANTING

Mesh Stitch

Row 1 (WS): K2, [yo, ssk] to last st, k1.

Row 2 (RS): Knit.

Repeat **Rows 1 & 2** until scarf measures 30in/76cm from turning point, ending with a **RS** row.

Next Row (Inc Row): K1, kfb, [k3, kfb] 3 times, k4, [kfb, k3] 3 times, k2tog, k1. 39 sts

Next Row (RS): Knit.

Garter Stitch

Row 1 (WS): K1, kfb, knit to last 3 sts, k2tog, k1.

Row 2 (RS): Knit.

Repeat **Rows 1 & 2** until scarf measures 36in/91.5cm from turning point, ending with a **RS** row.

BO loosely. Wet block scarf to given measurements.

Arbutus

This structural cowl with its unique construction, uses short rows and subtle shaping to create the illusion of volume with just one skein of yarn. Knit in the round from the top down, these three tiers create a stacked effect mimicking the look of a double wrapped cowl. A slightly looser gauge creates a light and springy fabric that is easy to wear and perfect for any season.

Gauge

18 sts and 24 rows = 4in/10cm in St st

Yarn

1 skein Madelinetosh Tosh DK (100% superwash merino wool, 225yds/205m), shown in Sequoia [DK]

Needles

5mm/US8 circular needle, 16in

Notions

2 contrasting stitch markers
Yarn needle

Finished Measurements

Circumference
Top Tier: 17.75in/45cm
Middle Tier: 20in/51cm
Bottom Tier: 22.25in/56.5cm

Height: approximately 7in/18cm at back neck.

Stitch Guide

Wrap & Turn: Slip the next stitch purlwise, bring the yarn to the front (or back on purl rows), return the slipped stitch to the LH needle and bring the yarn to the back (or front on purl rows), turn the work and continue as directed. Knit or purl into the wrap as well as the stitch when you reach these wrapped stitches on the following rnd.

DIRECTIONS

Using cable method and 16in circular needle, CO 48 sts, pm (this marker will be referred to as **mid marker**), CO 32 more, pm (this marker will be referred to as **end of rnd**). Join for working in the rnd, being careful not to twist.

TOP TIER

Rnds 1 & 2: Purl to end of rnd.

Rnd 3: Knit to last st of rnd, **Wrap & Turn**.

Rnd 4 (WS): Purl to st before mid marker, **Wrap & Turn**.

Rnd 5 & 6: Knit to end of rnd.

Rnds 7-9: Purl to end of rnd.

Rnds 10-25: Repeat **Rnds 3-9** twice more, then work **Rnds 3-4** once more.

Rnd 26: Knit to last 3 sts of rnd, because the next rnd will be a knit rnd, hold yarn in front then **Wrap & Turn**.

Rnd 27 (WS): Knit to 3 sts before mid marker, **Wrap & Turn**.

Rnd 28: Purl to 5 sts before end of rnd, **Wrap & Turn**.

Rnd 29 (WS): BO knitwise until 5 sts remain before mid marker (4 sts on LH needle + 1 st on RH needle), p4, sm, purl to last 3 sts of rnd (remembering to pick up wraps of previous short rows), with yarn in back **Wrap & Turn**.

Rnd 30: Purl to mid marker, sm, p5,

using cable method CO 32 sts, join being careful not to twist, p5.

MIDDLE TIER

Purl 2 rnds.

Repeat **Rnds 3-9** of *Top Tier* three times, then work **Rnds 3-4** once more.

Repeat Rnds 26-29 of *Top Tier*.

Next Rnd: Purl to mid marker, sm, p5, using cable method CO 42 sts, join being careful not to twist, p5.

BOTTOM TIER

Rnd 1 & 2: Purl to end of rnd.

Rnd 3: Knit to last st of rnd, **Wrap & Turn**.

Rnd 4 (WS): Purl to last st before mid marker, **Wrap & Turn**.

Rnd 5: Knit to end of rnd.

Rnd 6: Knit to mid marker, sm, k3, m1, knit to last 3 sts of rnd, m1, k3.

Rnds 7-9: Purl to end of rnd.

Repeat **Rnds 3-9** of *Bottom Tier* four times more, then **Rnds 3-8** once more.

BO all sts purlwise, loosely.

Break yarn and weave in ends.

Grace

A fresh and retro take on an effortlessly classic raglan cardigan. A semi-fitted design with a soft rounded neck and subtle waist shaping to flatter any figure. Simple lace along the yoke ends just above the bust for a modestly feminine touch. Knit at a slightly looser gauge that gives elasticity to the fabric. Fingering weight yarn results in a beautifully light weight cardigan that is suited for almost any season and ideal for layering.

Gauge

24 sts and 32 rows = 4in/10cm in St st

Yarn

Sweet Georgia Yarns BFL Sock (80% superwash Bluefaced Leicester wool/20% nylon, 365m/400yds to 115g/4oz), shown in deep olive [fingering]

Needles

3.5mm/US4 circular needle, 32in
3.5mm/US4 dpns

Notions

4 stitch markers
Waste yarn
Yarn needle
10 small buttons (approx 0.5in/1.5cm)

HOW TO USE THIS PATTERN:

This cardigan is knit from the top down. To offer a wide range of sizes and maintain readability, this pattern is written with blank spaces so that you may input only the information pertaining to your size. Here is how to use this pattern:

1. Choose Your Size

Refer to the **Finished Measurements & Yarn Requirements** chart on page 54. Select your size based on the **To Fit Bust** measurements found at the top of the chart. If you prefer a looser or tighter fit choose a different size, using the *Finished Measurements* listed to guide you (sample is shown in size 34).

2. Find Your Size

Refer to the **Pattern Chart** on pages 52 & 53. Mark or highlight the column that contains the instructions for the size you have chosen.

3. Fill In The Blanks

Pencil in the numbers given in the **Pattern Chart** with the corresponding letters in the written pattern. Measurements are listed in inches and centimeters and larger spaces are provided so that you may include the unit of measurement within the space.

DIRECTIONS

YOKE

Using long tail method and circular needle CO (A)_____ sts.

Set Up Row: P1, pm, purl (B)_____, pm, purl (C)_____, pm, purl (B)_____, pm, p1.

Row 1 (RS): Kfb, sm, k1, m1, knit to last st before marker, m1, k1, sm, m1, k1, [yo, k2tog] to last st before marker, k1, m1, sm, k1, m1, knit to last st before marker, m1, k1, sm, kfb.

Row 2 (WS): Purl.

Row 3: Knit to marker, m1, sm, k1, m1, knit to last st before marker, m1, k1, sm, m1, [k2tog, yo] to marker, m1, sm, k1, m1, knit to last st before marker, m1, k1, sm, m1, knit to the end of row.

Row 4: Purl.

Row 5: K1, [yo, k2tog] to marker, m1, sm, k1, m1, knit to last st before marker, m1, k1, sm, m1, k1, [yo, k2tog] to last st before marker, k1, m1, sm, k1, m1, knit to last st before marker, m1, k1, sm, m1, [k2tog, yo] to last st, k1.

Row 6: Purl.

Row 7: K1, [k2tog, yo] to last st before marker, k1, m1, sm, k1, m1, knit to last st before marker, m1, k1, sm, m1, [k2tog, yo] to marker, m1, sm, k1, m1, knit to last st before marker, m1, k1, sm, m1, k1, [yo, k2tog] to last st, k1.

Row 8: Purl.

Rows 9-12: Repeat **Rows 5-8** once more.

Neck Shaping

Row 13: Kfb, [yo, k2tog] to marker, m1, sm, k1, m1, knit to last st before marker, m1, k1, sm, m1, k1, [yo, k2tog] to last st before marker, k1, m1, sm, k1, m1, knit to last st before marker, m1, k1, sm, m1, [k2tog, yo] to last st, kfb.

Row 14: Purl.

Row 15: K2, [k2tog, yo] to last st before marker, k1, m1, sm, k1, m1, knit to last st before marker, m1, k1, sm, m1, [k2tog, yo] to marker, m1, sm, k1, m1, knit to last st before marker, m1, k1, sm, m1, k1, [yo, k2tog] to last 2 sts, k2.

Row 16: Purl.

Row 17: Kfb, k1, [yo, k2tog] to marker, m1, sm, k1, m1, knit to last st before marker, m1, k1, sm, m1, k1, [yo, k2tog] to last st before marker, k1, m1, sm, k1, m1, knit to last st before marker, m1, k1, sm, m1, [k2tog, yo] to last 2 sts, k1, kfb.

Row 18: Purl.

Row 19: Kfb, [k2tog, yo] to last st before marker, k1, m1, sm, k1, m1, knit to last st before marker, m1, k1, sm, m1, [k2tog, yo] to marker, m1, sm, k1, m1, knit to last st before marker, m1, k1, sm, m1, k1, [yo, k2tog] to last st, kfb.

Row 20: Purl.

Row 21: Repeat **Row 17**.

Row 22: Purl.

Row 23: Repeat **Row 19**.

Row 24: Pfb, purl to last st pfb.

Row 25: Kfb, [k2tog, yo] to marker, m1, sm, k1, m1, knit to last st before marker, m1, k1, sm, m1, k1, [yo, k2tog] to last st before marker, k1, m1, sm, k1, m1, knit to last st before marker, m1, k1, sm, m1, [yo, k2tog] to last st, kfb.

Row 26: Pfb, purl to last st, pfb, using backwards loop method, CO (D)_____ sts.

Next Row: K1, [k2tog, yo] to marker, m1, sm, k1, m1, knit to last st before marker, m1, k1, sm, m1, [k2tog, yo] to marker, m1, sm, k1, m1, knit to last st before marker, m1, k1, sm, m1, k1, [yo, k2tog] to end of row, using backwards loop method, CO (D)_____ sts.

Next Row: Purl.

Continue Raglan Shaping

Next Row: K1, [yo, k2tog] to last st before marker, k1, m1, sm, k1, m1, knit to last st before marker, m1, k1, sm, m1, k1, [yo, k2tog] to last st before marker, k1, m1, sm, k1, m1, knit to last st before marker, m1, k1, sm, m1, k1, [k2tog, yo] to last st, k1.

Next Row: Purl.

Next Row: K1, [k2tog, yo] to marker, m1, sm, k1, m1, knit to last st before marker, m1, k1, sm, m1, [k2tog, yo] to marker, m1, sm, k1, m1, knit to last st before marker, m1, k1, sm, m1, [yo, k2tog] to last st, k1.

Repeat last 4 rows until there are:

(E)_____ front sts, (F)_____ sts each sleeve, (G)_____ back sts. (H)_____ total yoke sts.

Sizes 30, 34, 36, 38, 46, 48, and 50 Only:

Next Row: K1, [yo, k2tog] to last st before marker, k1, sm, knit to marker, sm, k1, [yo, k2tog] to last st before marker, k1, sm, knit to marker, sm, k1, [k2tog, yo] to last st, k1.

Next Row: Purl

Next Row: K1, [k2tog, yo] to last st before marker, k1, sm, knit to marker, sm, k1, [k2tog, yo] to last st before marker, sm, k1, [yo, k2tog] to last st, k1.

Next Row: Purl

Repeat last 4 rows until sleeves measure (I)_____ from CO edge, ending with a RS row.

Sizes 32, 40, 42, and 44 Only:

Next Row: K1, [k2tog, yo] to marker, sm, knit to marker, sm, [k2tog, yo] to marker, sm, knit to marker, sm, [yo, k2tog] to last st, k1.

Next Row: Purl

Next Row: K1, [yo, k2tog] to marker, sm, knit to marker, sm, [yo, k2tog] to marker, sm, knit to marker, sm, [k2tog, yo] to last st, k1.

Next Row: Purl

Repeat last 4 rows until sleeves measure (I)_____ from CO edge, ending with a RS row.

All Sizes:

Next WS Row (Separate sleeves from body): *Purl to marker, remove first marker, place (F)_____ sleeve sts onto waste yarn, remove second marker, using backwards loop method, CO (J)_____ sts, placing a marker at center of CO sts, repeat from * once more, purl to end of row.

BODY

Next Row: [Knit (K)_____ , m1] (L)_____ times, knit to marker, sm, knit (N)_____, [k3, m1] (O)_____ times, knit (N)_____, sm, knit (M), [m1, knit (K)_____] (L)_____ times.

(P)_____ total body sts.

Work in St st until garment measures 3in/7.5cm from CO sts at underarm.

Waist Shaping

Next Row (Dec Row): *Knit to 3 sts before marker, ssk, k1, sm, k1, k2tog, repeat from * once more, knit to end of row.

Continue in St st, working **Dec Row** every 2in/5cm twice more.

(Q)_____ total body sts.

Work in St st until cardigan measures (R)_____ from CO sts at underarm.

Hip Shaping

Next Row (Inc Row): *Knit to 1 st before marker, m1, k1, sm, k1, m1, repeat from * once more, knit to end of row.

Continue in St st, working **Inc Row** every 2in/5cm twice more.

(P)_____ total body sts.

Ribbing Setup Row: Work in **1 x 1 Ribbing** [k1, p1] to approx center back, m1, [p1, k1] to end of row.

Continue in **1 x 1 Ribbing** for 2in/5cm.

BO very loosely in rib.

Sleeves

Place (F)_____ sleeve sts onto dpns. Rejoin yarn, pick up and knit (J)_____ sts along CO edge of underarm, placing a marker at center of cast on stitches to denote beg of rnd. Join.

(S)_____ total sleeve sts.

Knit for 3in/7.5cm from underarm.

Next Rnd (Dec Rnd): K1, k2tog, knit to last 3 sts of rnd, ssk, k1.

Work **Dec Rnd** every (T)_____ until (U)_____ sleeve sts remain.

Work even until sleeve measures (V)_____ from underarm.

Work in **1 x 1 Ribbing** for 3in/7.5cm.

BO loosely in rib.

FINISHING

Right Buttonband

Beginning at bottom right corner of front, pick up and knit (W)_____ sts.

Knit 3 rows.

Next Row (Buttonhole Row): K2, *k2tog, yo twice, k2tog tbl, knit (X)_____, repeat from * 7 times more, k2tog, yo twice, k2tog tbl, knit to end of row.

Next Row: Knit across row, at each buttonhole knit Into the first yarn over then knit into the back of the second.

Knit 1 row. BO.

Left Buttonband

Beginning at top left corner of front, pick up and knit (W)_____ sts.

Knit 6 rows. BO.

Collar

Beginning at top right neck edge, pick up and knit (Y)_____ sts as follows:

5 sts along right buttonband,
(Z)_____ sts up right front neck,
(B)_____ sts along top of right sleeve,
(AA)_____ sts along back neck,
(B)_____ sts along top of left sleeve,
(Z) sts down left front neck, and 5 sts along left buttonband.

Knit 3 rows.

Next RS Row (Buttonhole Row): K1, k2tog, yo twice, k2tog tbl, knit to end of row.

Next Row: Knit across row, at buttonhole knit into the first yarn over then knit into the back of the second.

Knit 1 row.

BO tightly.

Sew buttons to left front button band corresponding with buttonholes. Weave in ends. Block garment according to schematic measurements listed on page 54 & 55.

To Fit Bust	in	30	32	34	36	38	40	42	44	46	48	50
	cm	76	81.5	86.5	91.5	96.5	102	107	112	117	122	127
Yoke												
A	Cast On	48	48	54	54	54	56	56	56	58	58	58
B	Sleeve (each sleeve)	10	10	12	12	12	12	12	12	12	12	12
C	Back Neck	26	26	28	28	28	30	30	30	32	32	32
D	Cast On for Front Neck	1	1	3	3	3	5	5	5	5	5	5
Continue Raglan Shaping												
E	Front Stitches (each side)	26	27	30	32	34	37	39	41	42	44	46
F	Sleeve (each sleeve)	42	44	48	52	56	58	62	66	68	72	76
G	Back Stitches	58	60	64	68	72	76	80	84	88	92	96
H	Total Yoke Stitches	194	202	220	236	252	266	282	298	308	324	340
I	Raglan Depth in	6.5	6.75	7	7.25	7.5	7.75	8	8.25	8.5	8.75	9
	cm	16.5	17	18	18.5	19	19.5	20.5	21	21.5	22	23
J	Cast On at Underarm	10	12	12	12	14	14	16	16	16	18	18
Body												
K	Increase Interval (front)	3	2	3	3	2	3	3	3	3	3	2
L	Stitches to Increase (front)	8	11	10	10	12	11	11	13	14	14	16
M	Stitches to Knit (front)	7	11	6	8	17	11	14	10	8	11	23
N	Stitches to Knit (back)	10	6	8	7	10	9	9	11	10	13	12
O	Stitches to Increase (back)	16	20	20	22	22	24	26	26	28	28	30
P	Total Body Stitches (bust/hips)	162	180	188	198	214	224	238	250	260	272	286

To Fit Bust		in	30	32	34	36	38	40	42	44	46	48	50
		cm	76	81.5	86.5	91.5	96.5	102	107	112	117	122	127
Shaping														
Q	Total Body Stitches (waist)		150	168	176	186	202	212	226	238	248	260	274
R	Work Even	in	11	11	11	11	10.75	10.75	10.5	10.5	10.25	10.25	10
		cm	28	28	28	28	27.5	27.5	26.5	26.5	26	26	25.5
Sleeve														
S	Total Sleeve Stitches		52	56	60	64	70	72	78	82	84	90	94
T	Decrease Round Interval	in	5.25	5.5	2.75	2	1.25	1.5	1	1	0.75	0.75	0.75
		cm	17	13	13.5	6.5	5	3	3.5	2.5	2.5	1.5	1.5
U	Total Sleeve Stitches		46	50	50	52	52	56	56	58	58	62	62
V	Work Even	in	14.5	15	15	15	15	15.5	15.5	15.5	15.5	16	16
		cm	37	38	38	38	38	39.5	39.5	39.5	39.5	40.5	40.5
Buttonband														
W	Pick Up Stitches for Buttonband		114	116	118	120	120	120	120	122	122	124	124
X	Stitches Between Buttonholes		9	9	9	9	9	9	9	10	10	10	10
Collar														
Y	Total Picked Up Stitches for Collar		124	124	136	136	136	145	145	145	148	148	148
Z	Pick Up Along Front Neck		29	29	32	32	32	35	35	35	35	35	35
AA	Pick Up Along Back Neck		36	36	38	38	38	41	41	41	44	44	44

To Fit Bust	in	30	32	34	36	38	40	42	44	46	48	50
	cm	76	81.5	86.5	91.5	96.5	102	106.5	112	117	122	127
Yarn Requirements												
Number of 115g skeins (365m/400yds)		2	3	3	3	3	3	3	4	4	4	4
Meters Required		699	781	828	882	957	1012	1082	1144	1184	1268	1330
Yards Required		766	856	908	967	1049	1109	1185	1254	1297	1389	1458
Finished Measurements (in)												
A	Bust/Hip Circumference	27.25	30.25	31.5	33.25	35.75	37.5	39.75	41.75	43.5	45.5	47.75
B	Body Length	23.5	23.75	24	24.25	24.25	24.5	24.5	24.75	24.75	25	25
C	Arm Circumference	8.75	9.25	10	10.75	11.75	12	13	13.75	14	15	15.75
D	Sleeve Length (from underarm)	17.5	18	18	18	18	18.5	18.5	18.5	18.5	19	19
E	Raglan Depth	6.5	6.75	7	7.25	7.5	7.75	8	8.25	8.5	8.75	9
F	Back Neck	5.75	5.75	6.25	6.25	6.25	6.75	6.75	6.75	7	7	7
G	Waist Circumference	25.25	28.25	29.5	31.25	33.75	35.5	37.75	39.75	41.5	43.5	45.75
Finished Measurements (cm)												
A	Bust/Hip Circumference	70	76.5	80	84	91	95	101	106	110.5	115.5	121.5
B	Body Length	59.5	60.5	61	61.5	61.5	62	62	63	63	63.5	63.5
C	Arm Circumference	22	23.5	25.5	27	29.5	30.5	33	34.5	35.5	38	40
D	Sleeve Length (from underarm)	44.5	45.5	45.5	45.5	45.5	47	47	47	47	48.5	48.5
E	Raglan Depth	16.5	17	18	18.5	19	19.5	20.5	21	21.5	22	23
F	Back Neck Width	14.5	14.5	16	16	16	17	17	17	18	18	18
G	Waist Circumference	65	71.5	75	79	86	90	96	101	105.5	110.5	116.5

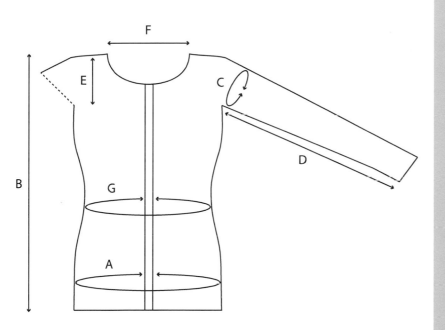

approx	approximately
beg	beginning
BO	bind off
CO	cast on
dec	decrease
dpns	double pointed needles
Inc	increase
k	knit
kfb	knit through front and back
k2tog	knit 2 together
LH	left hand
m1	make one
p	purl
pfb	purl through front and back
pm	place marker
psso	pass slipped st over
p2tog	purl 2 together
rem	remaining
RH	right hand
rnd(s)	round(s)
RS	right side
skp	slip 1, k1, psso
sk2p	slip 1, k2tog, psso
sl	slip
sm	slip marker
sp2p	slip 1, p2tog, psso
ssk	slip, slip, knit slipped sts together
st(s)	stitch(es)
St st	Stockinette stitch
tbl	through back loop
WS	wrong side
wyif	with yarn in front
yo	yarn over

Sweet Georgia Yarns

110-408 East Kent Avenue South

Vancouver, BC V5X 2X7

Canada

604.569.6811

sweetgeorgiayarns.com

Urban Yarns

4437 West 10 Avenue

Vancouver, BC V6R 2H8

604.228.1122

urbanyarns.com

Quince & Co.

info@quinceandco.com

quinceandco.com

Valley Yarn

valleyyarn.com

RESOURCES

THANK YOU

Shannon Cook for lending me your inspirations, effortless graphic talents, and valuable time. Thank you for the late night meetings, endless phone calls, countless emails, and thank you for pouring your heart into this as if the patterns were your own. I couldn't have done it without you!

Nicholas Kupiak for allowing me to create an entire collection based on your involvement. You are incredibly talented and I can't imagine handing this project to anyone but you. I trust your creative direction infinitely and am incredibly proud to have you as a brother.

Kylee Shaw for your enthusiasm modeling my samples, and for looking effortlessly beautiful doing it. Thank you for taking my instruction to heart and for doing an incredible job of styling the pieces, I couldn't have asked for more.

Katherine Vaughan for doing an amazing job as technical editor. I'm always astounded at how you are able to make minor adjustments that make a *world* of difference. Your final word gives me great confidence in my written patterns.

Felicia Lo of Sweet Georgia Yarns for dyeing up a special batch of BFL Sock in Deep Olive for the Grace cardigan. The yarn is such a huge element of the design process and it's always a pleasure to work with yours.

Anina, Alexa, Kynna and all of the amazing knitters at Urban Yarns for their encouragement, and for stocking the best selection of Madelinetosh Vintage and DK that I have ever encountered. Obviously this collection would have turned out very differently if it weren't for you lovely enablers.

Julie Verzosa of Valley Yarn Ltd for bringing your amazing selection of yarns to Fibres West. The skeins for Rathtrevor & Arbutus came from your fantastic booth.

Quince & Co. for creating truly inspirational yarn. Strathcona deserved nothing less than to be designed with your heavenly Sparrow.

The knitters in my life for their endless encouragement, support, and enthusiasm for my work. None of this would be possible without you!

RENFREW
page 40

RATHTREVOR
page 42

DIRECTORY

STRATHCONA
page 44

ARBUTUS
page 46

GRACE
page 48

FIVE ORIGINAL
DESIGNS

hat
fingerless gloves
cardigan
scarf
cowl

ABOUT THE AUTHOR

Jane lives and works from her home on Vancouver Island. She has been self publishing her designs since 2008, and most recently has been published in Knitty and November Knits (Interweave Press 2012).

Known for her classic aesthetic and clearly written patterns, Jane delivers designs that are fun to knit and easy to wear.

website : janerichmond.com
ravelry : ravelry.com/designers/jane-richmond
etsy : janerichmond.etsy.com
facebook : facebook.com/JaneRichmondDesigns
twitter : twitter.com/jane_richmond_
email : janerichmonddesigns@gmail.com